I can find JESUS in this book.
I will keep looking for him in my life.

JOSEPH TRANGONE

(NAME)

can you find JESUS?

Introducing Your Child to the Gospel

Written by **Philip D. Gallery**

Illustrated by **Janet L. Harlow**

NOVALIS

ST. ANTHONY MESSENGER PRESS

Cincinnati, Ohio

CASSELL

In praise of Our Father,
who art in Heaven

Written by Philip D. Gallery
Illustrated by Janet L. Harlow
Cover design by Tin Box Studio
Book design by Mary Alfieri
Design assistance by David A. Juergens/RPI

Copyright ©1996, Philip D. Gallery and Janet L. Harlow

Published in the United States by
St. Anthony Messenger Press
1615 Republic St., Cincinnati, OH 45210-1298

ISBN 0-86716-270-8

Published in Canada by Novalis
49 Front St. E, 2nd Floor,
Toronto, Ontario M5E 1B3 Canada

Canadian Cataloguing in Publication Data
Gallery, Philip D
  Can you find Jesus?: introducing your child to the Gospel
ISBN 2-89088-782-0

  1. Jesus Christ—Biography—Juvenile literature.
  2. Jesus Christ—Biography—Pictorial works—Juvenile.
  I. Harlow, Janet L. II. Title

BT302.G35 1996   j232.9'01   C96-900518-0

First published in the United Kingdom by Cassell
Wellington House, 125 Strand, London WC2R 0BB
127 W. 24th St., 4th Floor, New York, NY 10011

First published 1996

British Library Cataloguing-in-Publication Data
A catalogue record for this book is available from the
British Library.

ISBN 0-304-33968-7

Printed and bound in the U.S.A. by Quebecor

Contents

Introduction

To help your child learn about Jesus, we drew a picture journey through his life. All you have to do is guide the search for Jesus and other people from the Bible. As you search the pictures together, your child will learn about Jesus and many of the most important things he did.

While young children can learn and have fun with our book on their own, the presence of a parent, a grandparent, teacher or friend—*your* presence—enables them to learn even more about Jesus.

To help you in your search for Jesus, you will find at the back of the book a Parent's Guide for each picture. These guides are full of information about Jesus that your child can discuss with you. The guides will help you develop a fuller understanding of the life and teachings of Jesus. We encourage you to read the guide before beginning to explore the picture with your child. The recommended Scripture readings and discussion outlines will fill out the story depicted by the drawings and fill in the story between the images.

Begin by reading the brief paragraph in the margin of each picture. Then read the Bible verses that introduce each search, allowing your child to complete each search as you go along. As you read, you will see some words, printed in italics, that may not be familiar to a child. You will find the meanings of these words in the Glossary on page 39.

For the adventurer in each of us, we have also hidden in every picture ten symbols associated with the life of Jesus. You and your child can discover these symbols by studying each picture carefully until you find a person or thing that appears in every one of them. If you need help, the symbols are revealed and explained in Hidden in Every Picture on page 4.

There is one more thing to look for. Some of the pictures have modern things in them—things that were not around in the time of Jesus. In other pictures we have added silly things we hope will make you laugh. Please watch for these and laugh about them together.

We hope you and your child will enjoy our book together and read it over and over. Happy hunting!

Philip Gallery and Janet Harlow

Hidden in Every Picture

These ten things are hidden in every picture. Nine of them hold special meaning in the life of Jesus and for Christians. The tenth one is *you*—and each of us.

 **Angels** are beings created by God to share the joy of heaven. God has often sent angels as messengers. An angel asked Mary to be the mother of Jesus. Angels sang at Jesus' birth. An angel told the women who were looking for Jesus at his tomb that he had risen. (See Search 1: "Jesus Is Born" and Search 11: "Jesus Returns to His Friends.")

 Bread was the most important food for the people when Jesus lived. Jesus often compared himself to bread to show how he gives life. He called himself "the bread of life." (See Search 6: "Jesus Teaches and Feeds His Followers" and Search 9: "Jesus Celebrates the Last Supper.")

 The **coin** of Caesar (money used when Jesus lived) is commonly used to symbolize the power of the world. The Jews in Jesus' time wouldn't allow a Roman coin in the Temple because the coins had on them a picture of the Roman emperor Caesar, who claimed to be a god. Jesus often warned that people who care too much for money may forget God. (See Search 2: "Jesus Begins His Father's Work.")

 The **cross** reminds us of how Jesus was crucified and died on a cross and how he saved us. (See Search 10: "Jesus Dies for Us.")

 A **crown** is a symbol of earthly power. Many of the followers of Jesus thought he was the promised Messiah, the king who would free the Jews from Roman rule. To make fun of Jesus and his followers, the soldiers made a crown out of thorn branches and forced it onto Jesus' head. (See Search 10: "Jesus Dies for Us.")

The **dove** represents peace and the Spirit of God. When Jesus came out of the Jordan River after being baptized by John the Baptist, people saw a dove over Jesus' head. (See Search 3: "Jesus Is Baptized.")

The **fish** stands for Christians. Jesus told his disciples that he would make them fishers of people, meaning that his disciples were to go out into the city and the country and tell everyone about Jesus. So when the disciples had to hide from people who wanted to hurt them, they chose the fish as their secret sign. (See Search 13: "Jesus Lives in Us.")

The **lamb** is the animal the Jews eat at the Passover meal to remember the night God freed them from slavery in Egypt. Jesus is called the "Lamb of God" because his death frees all people from the slavery of sin. (See Search 3: "Jesus Is Baptized.")

People threw **palm** branches on the road in front of Jesus as he entered Jerusalem before the Last Supper to show respect for the man they thought would soon be their king. Palm branches are used in some churches on the Sunday before Easter to help people remember Jesus' entry into Jerusalem. (See Search 8: "Jesus Enters Jerusalem.")

The **child** in modern clothes shows that Jesus wasn't someone just for the people of his day but is living today in all of us. (See Search 13: "Jesus Lives in Us.")

• SEARCH 1 •
Jesus Is Born

A long time ago God promised to send the Son into the world. When the time came for Jesus to come to us, God chose Mary and Joseph to be his parents on earth. Just before Jesus was born, Mary and Joseph went to *Bethlehem* to be counted in the *census*. When they got there all the inns were full, so they had to sleep in a *stable*.

There Mary gave birth to Jesus, wrapped him in *swaddling clothes* and laid him in a *manger*.
CAN YOU FIND JESUS?

Shepherds were out in the fields, watching over their sheep through the night. An angel of the *Lord* came and said to them, "A *Savior* is born to you today in the *city of David*—the *Messiah*, the Lord." **CAN YOU COUNT THE SHEEP?**

Suddenly the *heavenly host* appeared. Many angels praised God and sang, "Glory to God in the highest, and on earth peace among those God favors." **HOW MANY ANGELS CAN YOU SEE?**

After Jesus was born, three Wise Men came looking for him. They saw a new star in the sky and followed it until they found Jesus. **CAN YOU FIND THE WISE MEN?**

The star the Wise Men saw in the east went before them until it came over where the child was. When the Wise Men found Jesus, they gave him gifts of gold, *frankincense* and *myrrh*. **CAN YOU FIND THE STAR?**

DO NOT ENTER

OPEN ON DAY OF ATONEMENT ONLY!!

ALTAR SALE

Jesus Begins His Father's Work

Soon after Jesus was born, Mary and Joseph left *Bethlehem* and took Jesus home to *Nazareth*. Jesus helped his mother around the house and helped Joseph in his carpenter's shop. As Jesus grew, God, his heavenly Father, watched over him. Each year Jesus and his parents and a group of friends and relatives went to *Jerusalem* for the *Passover* celebration. While in Jerusalem, they would go to the *Temple* to listen to the *teachers* or *rabbis*. When Jesus was twelve, he stayed behind in Jerusalem to talk to the teachers in the Temple.

As Mary and Joseph were returning home at the end of the feast, they looked for Jesus among their traveling companions. Unable to find him and very worried, Mary and Joseph returned to Jerusalem to look for him. **CAN YOU FIND MARY AND JOSEPH?**

 On the third day they found Jesus in the Temple. **CAN YOU FIND THE TEMPLE?**

Jesus was sitting with the teachers, listening to them and asking them questions. **HOW MANY TEACHERS CAN YOU FIND?**

Mary and Joseph were surprised when they saw Jesus. Mary said to him, "Why have you made us worry about you? Your father and I have been looking everywhere for you." **CAN YOU FIND JESUS?**

Jesus answered, "Why were you searching for me? Didn't you know that I had to be in my Father's house?" **WHERE IS THE FATHER'S HOUSE?**

9

•SEARCH 3•

Jesus Is Baptized

Jesus helped Mary and Joseph until he was about thirty years old. Then he began the public work God had sent him to do. First, he *dedicated* his life to God, his heavenly Father, by going to *John the Baptist* to be *baptized*. When John saw Jesus coming, he said, "Here is the *Lamb of God* who takes away the sin of the world!" John called Jesus the Lamb of God to compare him to the lambs the Jewish people offered to God and ate for their Passover dinner.

 John wore clothing of camel's hair with a leather belt around his waist and ate locusts and wild honey. **HOW MANY LOCUSTS AND BEEHIVES CAN YOU COUNT?**

The people were questioning in their hearts if John was the *Messiah*. But John told them, "I baptize you with water; but one who is more powerful is coming to baptize you with the *Holy Spirit*." **CAN YOU FIND JOHN?**

Jesus came to John to be baptized. John told him, "I should be baptized by you." Jesus replied that John had to baptize him because God wanted him to. Jesus then walked into the river to be baptized. **CAN YOU FIND JESUS?**

After Jesus was baptized, the *Spirit of God* came down on Jesus in the form of a dove. A voice from heaven said, "You are my Son, the Beloved; with you I am well pleased." **CAN YOU FIND THE SPIRIT OF GOD?**

Jesus Performs His First Miracle

One day Mary, Jesus and his *disciples* were all invited to the *marriage* of two of his friends. Before the celebration was over, Mary noticed that the *wedding* couple had run out of wine. Mary asked Jesus to help his friends. Because Jesus loved his mother and his friends, and because he thought it was important to *celebrate* a marriage, he did help by changing water into wine.

 Jesus, his mother and his disciples went to a wedding at Cana in *Galilee*. **CAN YOU FIND THE WEDDING COUPLE?**

When the servers ran out of wine, Mary said to Jesus, "They have no more wine." Jesus replied, "What does that matter to me? *My hour* has not yet come." **CAN YOU FIND MARY?**

But Mary told the waiters, "Do whatever Jesus tells you." There were six stone water jars in the room. Jesus told the waiters, "Fill those jars with water." **CAN YOU COUNT THE JARS?**

Then Jesus said, "Take some of the water out of a jar to the waiter in charge." The waiter in charge tasted it. It was wine! He said to the groom, "People usually serve good wine first, but you have kept the best until now." **CAN YOU FIND THE WAITER IN CHARGE?**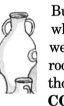

Jesus performed this first *miracle* at Cana in Galilee. In this way he showed his power, and the disciples believed in him. **CAN YOU FIND JESUS?**

13

•SEARCH 5•

Jesus Heals the People

The main reason Jesus came to the world was to show us how much God loves us. Jesus did this by healing many people who were sick and by performing other miracles.

A man who couldn't walk was lowered to Jesus from a rooftop. "Pick up your mat," Jesus said. The man stood up and walked outside. **CAN YOU FIND THE MAN ON THE MAT?**

A man who could not hear and who also had trouble talking came to Jesus. Jesus put his fingers into the man's ears and touched his tongue. Then Jesus looked up to *heaven* and said, "Be opened!" At once the man could hear, and he began to speak plainly. **CAN YOU FIND JESUS?**

Lazarus, a friend of Jesus, died. Jesus came to his *tomb* and told the people, "Take the stone away." Jesus then called out loudly, "Lazarus, come out!" and Lazarus immediately appeared. **CAN YOU FIND LAZARUS?**

One day ten people with *leprosy* met Jesus. They raised their voices and begged, "Have pity on us!" Jesus told them, "Go and show yourselves to the *priests*." On their way to the priests the ten people were cured. **CAN YOU COUNT THE PEOPLE WITH LEPROSY?**

Some friends of Jesus were in a boat when they saw Jesus walking toward them across the water. Peter said, "Lord, if it is really you, tell me to walk across the water to you." Peter started to walk on the water, but he became frightened and started to sink. So Jesus reached out and caught him. **CAN YOU FIND PETER?**

14

4 DAYS IN TOMB

VILLAGE

BUSINESS

OIL & VIN

•SEARCH 6•

Jesus Teaches and Feeds His Followers

Jesus walked from village to village telling people God loves them. One day he taught a crowd of people ways to show God they love him. These teachings are now called the *Sermon* on the Mount. Some of the most important rules Jesus gave us are called the *Beatitudes*. They begin with the word *blessed*. People who live this way are special friends of God. When Jesus finished teaching, people were getting hungry, so he fed them.

 Jesus went up the mountain and began to teach a large crowd of people. **CAN YOU FIND JESUS?**

"Blessed are they who *mourn*, for they will be comforted." **CAN YOU FIND THE MOURNERS?**

"Blessed are they who hunger and thirst for *holiness*, for they will be filled." **CAN YOU FIND THE CHILDREN PRAYING?**

"Blessed are the *peacemakers*, for they shall be called children of God." **CAN YOU FIND THE PEACEMAKERS?**

When it was evening, Jesus told his disciples to give the people something to eat. All they had were five loaves of bread and a few fish. **CAN YOU FIND THE LOAVES AND FISH?**

Jesus looked toward heaven and blessed the loaves and fish. Then he gave them to the people. After everyone had eaten, twelve baskets of leftovers were collected. **HOW MANY BASKETS CAN YOU FIND?**

17

•SEARCH 7•

Jesus Calls the Little Children

The disciples of Jesus tried to keep the children away from him because the disciples thought the children were bothering him. But Jesus told his disciples to let the children come to him so he could bless them and hold them. Jesus knew the children could help him teach everyone how important and easy it is to love God. Children accept and give love with complete trust. They trust those who love them. And children demand nothing in return for their love. Jesus asks all of us to love God with the same total trust.

Little children were being brought to Jesus so that he might lay his hands on them and *pray*. **CAN YOU FIND THE PARENTS?**

People were even bringing infants to Jesus that he might touch them. **CAN YOU FIND THE BABY?**

The disciples of Jesus began to scold the parents for bothering Jesus. **CAN YOU FIND THE DISCIPLES?**

But Jesus said, "Let the children come to me and do not stop them. For the *Kingdom of God* belongs to children such as these. Whoever does not receive the Kingdom of God like a little child will never enter it. Then he picked them up in his arms and blessed them." **CAN YOU FIND JESUS?**

God is Great, God is Good
And we thank Him for our food.
Amen.

For the food of which we are about to receive, we thank thee, O Lord. Amen.

For health and strength and daily bread we praise thy name O Lord. Amen.

YES, JE-SUS LOVES ME.... YES, JE-SUS

♪ Jesus loves me, this I know,
For the Bible tells me so...
Little ones to him belong,
They are weak, but He is strong.

God bless Mommy,
God bless Daddy,
God bless......

Now I lay me down to sleep,
I pray the Lord my soul to keep.
If I should die before I wake,
I pray the Lord my soul to take. Amen.

•SEARCH 8•

Jesus Enters Jerusalem

After traveling for three years, teaching and healing, Jesus went to Jerusalem. As he neared the city, the people came out to greet him. They cheered and said they wanted to make him their king. Many people thought Jesus would be a king like the kings they already knew. But Jesus came into the world to be a king of peace and love. Jesus wants to change people's hearts.

Nearing Jerusalem, Jesus sent two disciples ahead. He told them, "Go into the village and you will find a *colt*. Untie it and bring it back to me." **CAN YOU FIND THE DISCIPLES?**

 So the disciples went off. They found the colt tied near a gate. They untied it to take it to Jesus. **CAN YOU FIND THE COLT?**

Then the disciples led the colt to Jesus. They laid their *cloaks* on it and helped Jesus get on. **CAN YOU FIND JESUS?**

 Many people spread their cloaks on the road, while others spread reeds and palm branches they had cut. **CAN YOU FIND THE MAN CUTTING THE BRANCHES?**

The crowd heard that Jesus was about to enter Jerusalem, so they got palm branches and came out to meet him. They kept shouting "*Hosanna* to the son of David! Blessed is the one who comes in the name of the Lord!
Blessed is the *King of Israel*!" **HOW MANY PEOPLE HOLDING PALM BRANCHES CAN YOU COUNT?**

21

•SEARCH 9•

Jesus Celebrates the Last Supper

Jesus went to the Temple to teach. Finding *money changers* using his Father's house as a marketplace, Jesus grew angry. He threw them out of the Temple, saying, "My house is supposed to be a house of *prayer*, but you are making it a den of robbers." After teaching, Jesus sent two disciples to find a place to eat the Passover meal. The meal they shared has come to be called the "Last Supper."

Jesus told the two disciples they would meet a man carrying a water jar. "Talk to the owner of the house he enters," Jesus said. "Tell him that the Teacher needs to eat the Passover in his guest room." **CAN YOU FIND THE MAN WITH THE WATER JAR?**

 During the meal, Jesus took bread, blessed it and gave it to his disciples. "Take this and eat it," he said. "This is my body." **CAN YOU FIND THE BREAD?**

Next, Jesus took a cup of wine. "Drink from it, all of you," he said, "for this is my blood, the blood of the *covenant* shed for the forgiveness of *sins*." **CAN YOU FIND THE CUP?**

Then Jesus told them, "One of you will *betray* me." **CAN YOU FIND JESUS?**

Jesus then passed some food to Judas. After eating it, Judas left. **CAN YOU FIND JUDAS?**

Then Peter said, "Lord, I will go with you to prison or to death." Jesus said "Peter, the rooster will not crow in the morning until you have three times denied that you know me." **CAN YOU FIND THE ROOSTER?**

When the Passover supper ended, Jesus and his disciples went into a garden to pray. As Jesus prayed, Judas, who had been paid thirty pieces of silver, showed Jesus' enemies where to find him. Jesus did not fight to escape. He wanted to show that it is better to love and forgive each other than to fight and hurt each other.

In the garden, Jesus prayed, "Father if you are willing, take this cup from me. But let your will, not mine, be done." Then a crowd came and led him away. **CAN YOU FIND JUDAS?**

Jesus was led to *Pilate*, who asked him, "Are you the king of the Jews?" **CAN YOU FIND PILATE?**

Pilate had Jesus beaten. The soldiers wove a *crown of thorns* and put it on Jesus' head. Then the soldiers led Jesus out to be *crucified*. **CAN YOU FIND JESUS?**

As they went out, they met a man named Simon. The soldiers made Simon help carry Jesus' cross. **CAN YOU FIND SIMON?**

At the *Place of the Skull* they crucified Jesus between two criminals. **CAN YOU FIND THE TWO CRIMINALS?**

After three hours, Jesus cried out, "Father, into your hands I commend my spirit." Then he died. A man named Joseph took Jesus down from the cross and laid him in a tomb. **CAN YOU FIND JOSEPH?**

Jesus Returns to His Friends

Three days after Jesus was buried, friends came to the tomb to clean his body. But Jesus was gone. In his place was a young man who told them Jesus had been raised from the dead.

Mary Magdalene, a friend of Jesus, saw a man standing behind her. He called, "Mary!" Hearing his voice, she knew it was Jesus.  **CAN YOU FIND JESUS WITH MARY?**

That same day two disciples were walking to the village of Emmaus. A man joined them, but they didn't know he was Jesus. The disciples asked the man to eat with them. When he blessed the bread, the disciples knew he was Jesus. Then they returned to Jerusalem to tell other friends. **CAN YOU FIND JESUS BLESSING THE BREAD?**

Later, Jesus appeared to the disciples in Jerusalem and said, "Peace be with you." **CAN YOU FIND JESUS WITH THE DISCIPLES?**

Thomas, who wasn't there, didn't believe Jesus had returned. Jesus came again and told Thomas to feel the nail holes in his hands. When Thomas saw Jesus he believed. Jesus said, "Do you believe just because you see me? Blessed are the people who have not seen me and still believe." **CAN YOU FIND JESUS WITH THOMAS?**

Jesus showed himself again to his disciples by the Sea of Tiberias. After they had eaten a picnic lunch, Jesus asked Peter, "Do you love me?" Peter answered, "Yes, Lord; you know that I love you." **CAN YOU FIND JESUS WITH PETER ON THE BEACH?**

•SEARCH 12•
Jesus Returns to His Father

To convince his friends he was really alive, Jesus visited them after he rose from the dead. He also wanted to help them become strong enough to go into the world to tell people about him. When it was time to leave them, Jesus returned to his Father in heaven, the Father who had sent him as a baby to the stable in Bethlehem.

Jesus called his disciples together on a mountain. When they arrived, Jesus told them, "Go and make disciples everywhere in the world, baptizing them in the name of the Father, the Son and the Holy Spirit. Teach them to do everything I have taught you. And I will be with you always." **CAN YOU FIND THE ELEVEN DISCIPLES?**

Then Jesus told them, "You will be my *witnesses* to the ends of the earth." Then he was lifted up and disappeared from their sight in a cloud. **CAN YOU FIND JESUS?**

As the disciples stood looking up at the sky, two men in white robes stood by them. "Why do you stand looking up toward heaven?" they asked. "Jesus has been taken from you into heaven. He will come back in the same way you saw him go." **CAN YOU FIND THE TWO MEN?**

Later, when the disciples were together, *tongues of fire* appeared. The flames separated and came to rest on each disciple. Each one of them was filled with the Holy Spirit. **HOW MANY TONGUES OF FIRE CAN YOU COUNT?**

Jesus Lives in Us

After Jesus returned to his Father in heaven, his disciples did what he had commanded: They went wherever they could to teach people about Jesus. They told everyone that God loves us and wants us to love God and each other. They taught that Jesus wants us to show our love for God by loving people, and that the best way to show that we love people is by helping them whenever we can.

The disciples told people about the day Jesus showed how important it is to help each other. The disciples said Jesus had taught them that if we help people during our lives, God will welcome us into heaven. Jesus said God would do this because whenever we help someone else, we are also helping God and showing our love for God.

While the disciples were teaching everyone how much God loves us, a man named Paul was hurting many of the people who loved Jesus. One day Jesus surprised Paul. Jesus asked him, "Paul, why are you hurting me?" Paul then asked, "Who are you, Lord?" Jesus answered, "I am Jesus, the one you are hurting." Paul then saw that whenever he hurt anyone, he was also hurting Jesus. After Paul understood this, he worked very hard to help people learn about Jesus.

Even though around two thousand years have passed since Jesus lived on earth, many people still go all over the world telling his story. They remind us that we should love one another as much as we love God. They also tell people that Jesus loves each of us and is a part of each of us.

Can you find

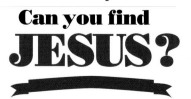

JESUS?

SEARCH 1

Jesus Is Born
Luke 2:1-14; Matthew 2:1-11

1) After looking over the picture, read 2 Samuel 7:12-17 with your child or tell the story in your own words. The prophet Nathan tells King David that God has promised that one of David's descendants will be special to God. Discuss the connection between these verses and the birth of Jesus in Bethlehem (see Micah 5:1-5), the city of David. Point out that Jesus is the fulfillment of the promise God made to David.

2) After finding Jesus in the manger, read Luke 1:26-38, where Mary is told by the angel Gabriel that she is to be the mother of Jesus. Emphasize Mary's willingness to do what God asks and discuss how each of us should be willing, as Mary was, to do what God asks.

3) After completing the searches, point out that after the census, Jesus returned home with Mary and Joseph (see Luke 2:39-40). Imagine some of the things Jesus may have done as a young child (to the age of twelve or so) to help around the house (cleaning, gathering firewood for cooking and heating, helping in the garden and with the animals, etc.). Return to the picture and locate children doing some of these tasks. Also discuss some things Jesus probably did to help in Joseph's carpentry shop (carrying, measuring, helping to saw wood, helping to build and deliver furniture). Compare these chores to the things your child does to help you.

4) Discuss how Jesus learned about his Jewish faith. Explain that Jesus was a Jew and, as such, was a descendant of Abraham (see Genesis 12:1-8). Point out that Jesus received religious training at home and also in his "church," which was called a synagogue. In the synagogue Jesus would have studied the Jewish holy writings and would have been instructed in his religion by men called *rabbis*, a word meaning "teacher." The next picture shows Jesus talking with the teachers in the Temple.

SEARCH 2

Jesus Begins His Father's Work
Luke 2:43-49

1) Before beginning to examine the picture, read Exodus 12:1-32 or tell the story in your own words. These verses detail the origin of the Passover celebration. Select the verses you think are most helpful to convey the story to your child.

2) After finding Jesus in the Temple, explain that the Temple was a place for the Jewish people to come together to pray to God and to study God's teachings. Point out that the Jewish Holy Book is what Christians know as the Old Testament of the Bible. Also note that today Jewish places of worship are usually called synagogues. Help your child understand that your church, in addition to being Jesus' house, is also his Father's house. Discuss with your child the kinds of worship, learning and activities that take place in your church.

3) When the teachers have been counted, explain that they were called *rabbis* and were men who had spent their lives studying the sacred Jewish writings—what we call the Old Testament. Their job was to preserve and pass on the history, traditions and religious beliefs of the Jewish people. Point out that there were few books, so most teaching was done orally. Finally, look at the ways you and your child try to preserve and pass on your religious traditions and beliefs (reading the Bible, praying together, attending church, visiting the sick, feeding the hungry). If possible, discuss with your pastor, director of religious education or pastoral agent how he or she came to be a "teacher."

4) After this episode in the Temple, the Bible story skips ahead about twenty years. With your child, try to imagine what kind of life Jesus led growing up. What sort of games did he play with his friends? Did his peers look up to him? Do you think he did things he wasn't supposed to do just because his friends wanted him to do them? Explain that in Jesus' day sons learned a skill from their fathers. So Jesus worked with Joseph in the carpentry shop to learn Joseph's trade and help support his family. He also studied with the teachers in the synagogue to learn about the work that God, his heavenly Father, wanted him to do.

SEARCH 3

Jesus Is Baptized
Matthew 3:4,13-15;
Luke 3:15-16; Mark 11:10-11

1) Before beginning to explore the picture, explain to your child that approximately twenty years have passed since Jesus last appeared in the Gospels. Discuss how, as a young man, Jesus might have spent his time—helping Joseph in his carpenter's shop by taking over more and more of the work as his father got older? Caring for sick relatives and friends (remember most people died before the age of forty)? Learning from the Jewish teachers? Spending time with friends? Compare the work Jesus most likely did to the work you do or your child might do as an adult. Try to make Jesus' life seem real to your child. Point out that, in this picture, Jesus is about thirty years old and has decided it is time for him to become a teacher himself.

2) After finding John the Baptist, tell your child the story of Luke 1:39-80 in your own words. Discuss John's relationship with Jesus, both as Jesus' cousin and as a man sent by God to urge people to turn away from evil and back to God. Consider why the people who met John might have thought he was the promised Messiah (see Isaiah 9:5-6; 11:1-5; Daniel 7:13-14). Discuss whether either of you has ever met someone like John—someone dedicated to working for God. (You can find more information about John the Baptist in Mark 1:1-8.)

3) When you have found Jesus, get out your child's baptismal candle, certificate, photographs and any other remembrances of the ceremony you may have. Share them with your child and tell why you felt it was important for him or her to be baptized. Remind your child who his or her godparents are and explain why you chose these people as godparents. Perhaps you could phone or visit the godparents with your child or help your child write them a letter.

4) Discuss the term *Lamb of God*. Explain that at Passover the Jews offer God a spotless lamb which everyone shares at a meal. Point out that the Gospel of John is saying that when Jesus dies on the cross, it will be as the perfect lamb being offered for the sins of the world (see Isaiah 53).

5) Talk about the Holy Spirit in our lives. Explain that God wants to share love with each of us and that the Holy Spirit will bring God's love to us if we want it. Talk about some loving people you know and why they are so loving. Is it an openness to God's Holy Spirit?

SEARCH 4

Jesus Performs His First Miracle
John 2:1-11

1) After looking briefly at the picture, read Genesis 15; 17:1-8 or tell the story in your own words. Explain to your child that a covenant is a two-way agreement between people or groups to do or not do certain things; give simple examples. Then discuss God's covenant with Abraham. Point out that a wedding ceremony is a covenant between a man and a woman before God.

2) After finding the wedding couple, describe a modern wedding ceremony and talk about the promises the bride and groom make. If possible, view with your child a videotape or photos of your own wedding. Note some ways married people show that they are living up to the covenant they have made with each other.

3) When you have finished the searches, point out in the picture the items that were common in Jewish wedding ceremonies. The bride is holding a cup of wine, which the bride and groom share to symbolize their life together. In the groom's hand is a scroll that is the marriage contract; it specifies the bride's dowry and the groom's duties to support and honor his wife. The bride and groom are standing beneath a cloth canopy called a *huppah* (pronounced who puh), which sets aside a sacred area in which the marriage ceremony takes place. The huppah also symbolizes that the married couple will live together under one roof.

4) When you have completed your examination of the picture, discuss the commitment Jesus made to us: to be with us, to love us and to guide us. Talk about some things Jesus expects us to do to show our commitment to him (loving God and one another and living accordingly).

SEARCH 5

Jesus Heals the People
Mark 2:3-12; 7:32-35;
John 11:1-44; Luke 17:12-14; Matthew 14:22-31

1) After looking over the page, talk about God's power to heal people's bodies. Explain that the God who has the power to create the universe out of nothing certainly has the power to heal us. Your child might ask you why God doesn't use this power to remove all suffering from the world. Explain why God can't do that until all the people in the world decide to love God and each other.

2) When you have found Jesus, point out to your child that Jesus often talked about our failure to listen to what God tells us to do. Explain that Jesus would like our ears to be "opened" so we will hear his word and our tongues "loosened" so we will speak plainly about his word.

3) After you have found Lazarus, explain that by raising Lazarus from the dead, Jesus showed God's power over death. He also foreshadowed his own resurrection and the happy resurrection of all people at the end of time.

4) When you have located Peter, point out that Peter didn't begin to sink until he began to lose faith in the power of God. Explain to your child that when we lose faith in God, we too begin to sink—into materialism or ourselves or even despair. Discuss some of the things we can do to develop and maintain our faith in God: Spend time with people of strong faith, read the Bible, attend church regularly, pray often, read inspirational books about men and women of faith. Finally, discuss ways you and your child can strengthen your faith by working together.

SEARCH 6

Jesus Teaches and Feeds His Followers
Luke 6:17;
Matthew 5:4, 6, 9; 14:15-17; 14:19-21

1) When you have found the mourners, look for the physically ailing who have come to Jesus to be healed. Should your child ask why God doesn't always cure the sick, say that while we may think that being cured of a sickness would be the best thing for us, only God knows what is really the best for us. Explain that God can heal our hearts and minds and souls as well as our bodies.

2) After finding the peacemakers, read Matthew 6:19-21 with your child. Make a list of earthly treasures and heavenly treasures. Discuss the relative values of the things on each list.

3) Our treatment of the Sermon on the Mount ends with the search for the peacemakers. If you wish to go into greater detail, read Matthew 5-7 (see 5:3-11 for the Beatitudes) and Luke 6:17-49. Choose passages best suited for your child to read and discuss.

4) After finding the loaves and fish, discuss the difficulty of getting food in Jesus' time (no supermarkets, no fast food outlets). Point out how important bread was to the people. Explain that when Jesus told the people that he was the "bread of life" (see John 6:35), they could easily understand that he was saying that he was the most important thing in life and that, just as bread sustains a person's body, he would sustain them.

5) Discuss the importance of letting Jesus "feed" us with his love. Jesus turned a little bit of food into enough to feed thousands of people. Point out that if we let Jesus "feed" us with his love, we will be able to love thousands of people. And even after we have loved thousands of people, like the people who still had food left over after eating, we will still have love left for more people.

SEARCH 7

Jesus Calls the Little Children
Matthew 19:13; Mark 10:13-15; Luke 18:15

1) Look at the picture and read the introductory paragraph. Ask your child to tell you why Jesus liked to have children come to him. Going back over the introductory paragraph, help your child understand that Jesus wanted the children near him to share God's love with them. Point out that Jesus liked the love the children offered him in return.

2) After finding the parents, ask if your child would like to have been brought to Jesus. Discuss some of the things you and other adults are doing to bring children to Jesus.

3) When you have found the disciples, ask if anything in your child's life may be interfering with getting close to Jesus. Let your child talk. You might review the Beatitudes and Ten Commandments to help. Point out that all of us do things that keep us from Jesus, but Jesus still loves us anyway.

4) After finishing the page, ask your child why Jesus said that the Kingdom of God belongs to those who are like children. Explain that Jesus wasn't saying that the Kingdom belongs only to children, but that it belongs to all who accept God's love as openly as children accept the love of their parents and all who love them.

5) Go back to the picture and help your child learn the prayers. Explain that the grace before meals, the bedtime prayer and the song are all types of prayer because each is addressed to God. Explain that prayers aren't just words that other people have written, they are anything you say to or do for God. Help your child compose some easy-to-remember prayers. They can be as simple as "Good morning, Jesus." Also help your child "hear" God. Then, help your child do something for God—write to a grandparent, visit a sick relative or friend, take some food to a soup kitchen.

SEARCH 8

Jesus Enters Jerusalem
Matthew 21:1-2, 9;
Mark 11:4, 8; Luke 19:35; John 12:12-13

1) After looking at the picture, read Zechariah 9:9 with your child. Zechariah said that the savior of the Jewish people would be riding on a colt and would be called a king.

2) Point out to your child that Jesus was entering Jerusalem for the Passover feast (review Exodus 12:1-28). Recall that the Passover was a celebration of the Jewish people's escape from slavery. For this reason, many people greeted Jesus with the hope that he would be the "King of Israel" who would help them escape from Roman domination (see Matthew 2:1-2).

3) When you have counted the people holding palms, read Psalm 118:26-29. Point out that the people used some of the psalmist's words to welcome Jesus. Also point out that on the Sunday before Easter we read the story of the day people waved palms to welcome Jesus to Jerusalem.

4) Finally, explain to your child that Jesus was entering Jerusalem on the day the Jews picked out the lamb they would offer to God on the Passover (see Exodus 12:3). Explain that Jesus would soon allow himself to be offered to God to take away the sins of all the people in the world. Go back to Search 3: Jesus Is Baptized (page 10) and review how John the Baptist called Jesus "The Lamb of God who takes away the sin of the world."

SEARCH 9

Jesus Celebrates the Last Supper
Mark 14:12-14; Matthew 26:26-28;
John 13:21, 26, 30; Luke 22:33-34

1) After looking over the page, review the history of the Passover with your child (see Exodus 12:1-32). Explain that Jews consider Passover as the night of redemption— the night they were freed from the Egyptians. Point out that Christians consider the Passion of Jesus, which begins with this Passover meal with his disciples and ends with his death, to bring us freedom from the power of sin and death.

2) After finding the cup, review the concept of covenant with your child. Discuss the covenant that God made with Abraham (see Genesis 15; 17:1-8) and point out other examples of covenants: between wife and husband, employer and employee, parents and children. Finally, discuss the covenant Jesus is talking about between himself and all of us. Explain that Jesus is saying that he will give his life as his part of the covenant and that in return he expects us to love one another.

3) When you've found the rooster, talk about Peter's denial of Jesus. Point out that those who had arrested Jesus were powerful people and that Peter was understandably afraid of them. Explain that later Peter was sorry that he had denied Jesus, that Jesus forgave Peter and that Peter spent the rest of his life telling people about Jesus. Finally, explain that everyone occasionally denies Jesus by doing things Jesus doesn't want us to do or by failing to do things Jesus does want us to do. But if we're sorry, Jesus will forgive us; just like Peter, we can go on to serve Jesus.

SEARCH 10

Jesus Dies for Us
Luke 22:41-54; 23:26-53;
John 18:33-37; 19:1-2; Matthew 27:32

1) After finding Judas, explain that in his prayer Jesus was asking his Father to allow him to escape the suffering and death he was soon to endure. Point out that Jesus ended his prayer by accepting that his Father's will should prevail. Discuss the appropriate section of the Lord's Prayer with your child ("...your will be done on earth..."). Finally, explain to your child that when we pray we should ask for the wisdom and strength to accept God's will.

2) When you have found Pilate, read John 18:33-37. Discuss Jesus' Kingdom with your child. Explain that anyone committed in mind and heart to Jesus is a member of the Kingdom. You might want to review the Beatitudes (Matthew 5:3-12) to discover some of the characteristics of someone who is committed to Jesus.

3) When you have found Jesus, explain that he was crucified for all of us, including Peter and Judas, who both betrayed him. Compare how Peter responded to his betrayal (Matthew 26:69-75) with how Judas reacted (Matthew 27:3-5). Peter sought forgiveness by weeping and went on to serve God, while Judas sank into despair and killed himself. Make clear to your child that Peter's response to failing Jesus is the one we should try to copy.

4) After locating Simon, discuss with your child the fact that we, like Jesus, have crosses to bear: injury, the loss of loved ones, pain and sickness, lack of love. Ask what crosses your child is bearing. Point out some people who can help carry them—you, God, friends, a pastor, a teacher.

5) After you finish examining the picture, remind your child that Jesus was crucified as the "Lamb of God who takes away the sin of the world" (see John 1:29). Review the Jewish concept of the Passover lamb (Exodus 12:21-27). Point out that Jesus' blood was shed to free people, once and for all, from sin.

SEARCH 11

Jesus Returns to His Friends
John 20:11-16; 24-29; 21:1, 15; Luke 24:13-36

1) After looking over the picture, discuss with your child the nature of God. Help your child to see God as the creative force behind all that exists. Explain to your child that the God who made the universe out of nothing is able to do anything—including giving life back to Jesus.

2) After finding Jesus with Thomas, discuss Jesus' words to Thomas: "Do you believe just because you see me? Blessed are the people who have not seen me and still believe." It was easy for Thomas to believe because he saw Jesus. Discuss with your child the difficulty we all have in believing in a Jesus we haven't seen. Point out that Jesus understands this difficulty and will help us believe if we ask him to.

3) When you have found Jesus with Peter, discuss the instructions Jesus gave him: "Feed my lambs." Explain that a lamb will follow wherever the shepherd leads. Talk about Jesus as the "Good Shepherd" (see John 10:1-16). Talk over with your child some of the ways you can work together as a family to build your trust in Jesus (praying or reading the Bible together). Next, talk about some of the things being a faithful follower of Jesus might lead you to do in order to carry out his request to feed his lambs (go to church, visit the sick, feed the hungry, show kindness to all people you meet and forgiveness to those who hurt you).

4) If you feel your child is old enough to understand, read Jesus' question about whether it was necessary for the Messiah to suffer (see Luke 24:26). Point out that our lives, too, are journeys through the world to glory and, just like Jesus, we will have to die before we enter our glory.

SEARCH 12

Jesus Returns to His Father
Matthew 28:16-20; Acts 1:8-11; 2:3-4

1) After finding the eleven disciples, talk with your child about what Jesus meant when he told them to go make disciples of all nations. Tell your child that being a Christian means being a disciple of Jesus. Point out that being a disciple of Jesus requires that you follow Jesus' command to make disciples of all nations. Finally, ask if your child has any questions about how Baptism makes you a disciple of Jesus. If so, you could review some of the material in the Parent's Guide for Search 3, "Jesus Is Baptized," on page 32.

2) When you have found Jesus, read Acts 2:1-39. Explain that the Holy Spirit came to the disciples and allowed them to do wonderful works for God. Explain that because the disciples of Jesus loved him, they were willing to let the Holy Spirit help them. The Holy Spirit will help us, too. Point out that we may not be able to do all the things the disciples could do, but that we will still be able to help teach others the things Jesus wants us all to know.

3) When you have completed the searches, point out that those in heaven are part of the heavenly host that was first mentioned in Search 1, "Jesus Is Born." Just as the angels celebrated the birth of Jesus, they are celebrating his return to heaven. The two old men represent Abraham and Moses—two of the greatest Old Testament prophets, who helped prepare the world for the arrival of Jesus. Explain that all those who love Jesus will one day be part of the heavenly host and will join with it in praising God.

SEARCH 13

Jesus Lives in Us
Matthew 25:31-46; Acts 9:33-36

1) After briefly looking at the picture, ask why your child thinks God loves him or her. Explain that the love God the Father and Jesus share with each other is the source of God's desire to create each of us. God made us because God loves us. Help your child understand that God knew and loved us before we were born and will love us all through our lives. Further explain that the most important goal of Christians is to learn to love each other just as God loves us. Finally, read and discuss Mark 12:28-34, Luke 10:25-37 and 1 John 4:7-21 with your child.

2) Explain to your child that the buildings along the horizon represent the architectural styles of all the world's civilizations. Point out the different types of buildings and discuss the various civilizations they symbolize, what part of the earth they inhabit, and so on.

3) Point out that the people in the illustration represent the many races and occupations of humanity. Try to identify as many as you can. Discuss some of the occupations with which your child is familiar. Assure your child that God loves all of the people in the picture.

4) Help your child locate the eleven disciples, who are scattered throughout the picture, perhaps looking out of place in their ancient dress. Explain that they represent the women, men and young people who are today carrying out the command of Jesus to bring his story to all the people in the world. Tell your child that all of us should help carry Jesus' story to all the earth.

Glossary

Baptize To clean and set apart for God. Water is used in the ceremony to show that the person being baptized is being cleansed by God and born again to God.

Beatitude A blessing or happiness. Jesus mentions several in the Sermon on the Mount. Jesus gave us ways to find happiness in life.

Bethlehem A small village a few miles from Jerusalem, where Jesus was born (see Micah 5:1-5).

Betray To deliver into the hands of an enemy.

Blessed Made happy or holy.

Celebrate To observe an important occasion with festivities, such as music, food and dancing. When a man and a woman marry, they publicly dedicate themselves to each other.

Census A counting of people. At certain times the ancient Roman government required all people to return to their hometowns to be counted. The purpose of the census was to keep track of how many people there were and to decide how much tax they should pay. Modern countries also count their citizens and ask them how old they are, what kind of work they do and where they live.

Christ "The Anointed One"; someone chosen for a particular purpose. Christians believe Jesus is the Son of God, who came to save us from sin.

City of David Bethlehem was the hometown of David's family. David was a king of Israel in ancient times. God told David that one of his descendants (a child, grandchild, great-grandchild...) would be God's Son (see 2 Samuel 7:12-17).

Cloak A loose, outer piece of clothing worn over other clothes.

Colt A young male horse or donkey. Jesus rode a young donkey into Jerusalem.

Covenant An agreement to do or not do certain things.

Crown of thorns Headpieces worn by kings and queens, usually made of gold. Because Jesus said he was a king (see John 18:36-37), the Roman soldiers put a crown made out of thorns on his head to make fun of him.

Crucified Put to death by being nailed or tied to a cross.

Cup Jesus used this word to stand for his suffering and death.

Day of Atonement (Yom Kippur) A Jewish holy day on which Jews ask God to forgive their sins. In the time of Jesus, the high priest would sacrifice a goat to God, then make offerings to God as an apology for the people's sins (see Leviticus 16:29-34).

Dedicate To set apart for a specific purpose. Jesus sets himself apart to serve God.

Denarius Ancient Roman coins made of silver. A small gold coin was worth twenty-five denarii.

Disciple A pupil or follower of a teacher. A person sent out on a special mission. Jesus chose twelve disciples to be special messengers to tell the world about him. These special messengers are called the apostles.

Frankincense A rare and expensive substance that is burned for its pleasing smell.

Galilee Province where Jesus lived and taught: a northern district in what is now Israel. Cana and Nazareth were towns in Galilee.

Heaven The name Christians give to our way of being with God together forever, even after death.

Heavenly host The word *host* can be used to mean a large crowd of people. The "heavenly host" are those who are gathered together with God in heaven, especially the angels.

Holiness Being like God: loving, forgiving, welcoming, pure.

Holy Spirit The active presence of God in our life; God's love shared with us.

Hosanna A shout of praise to God. A Hebrew word meaning "God save us."

Israel Another name for the Jewish people. Jacob, one of the great leaders of the early Jewish people, was given this name after wrestling with an angel (see Genesis 32:24-28). Also, the name of the country where the Jews lived.

Jerusalem The most holy city of the Jewish people. Jesus had to travel about sixty miles (one hundred kilometers) from his hometown of Nazareth to get to Jerusalem.

John the Baptist A holy man who called people to become God's friends by being baptized and by doing what God wants them to do.

King of Israel A title given Jesus by some of his followers, who were hoping for an earthly king to save them from the Romans.

Kingdom of God All the people, both on earth and in heaven, who love God.

Lamb of God In Jesus' time, Jews offered lambs to God and shared them as the Passover meal. When John called Jesus the Lamb of God, he was saying that Jesus was offering himself to God.

Leprosy A disease that eats away a person's skin.

Lord A person who has great power. God is often called "the Lord."

Manger A box or trough for hay for cattle or horses to eat.

Marriage A husband and wife love and take care of each other all their lives.

Mary Magdalene A woman who became a close friend of Jesus. Some people think she was once a great sinner.

Menorah A candlestick with room for seven or nine candles that is a traditional symbol of the Jewish religion.

Messiah The person sent by God to free the people. At the time of Jesus, many Jews were waiting for God to send them a king who would free them from their Roman rulers. Many Jews thought Jesus was this special person (see **Christ**).

Miracle An unusual event, such as water turning into wine, that goes against the laws of nature and is therefore considered to be caused by God.

Money changers Roman money had the likeness of the emperor on it. Since the emperor claimed to be a god, the Jews refused to use Roman money in the Temple. They therefore had money changers who would give coins without the emperor in exchange for Roman coins. These coins could be taken into the Temple and used to buy animals to sacrifice to God.

Mourn To feel sad or to express grief or sorrow. In the Beatitudes Jesus says people who feel this way will be comforted.

'My Hour' When Jesus used this term at Cana, he meant he was not ready to begin showing people that he was the Son of God. But because he loved his mother, Jesus helped his friends anyway.

Myrrh A pleasant-smelling substance used in perfumes. It was something special only rich people could afford.

Nazareth A small town sixty miles (one hundred kilometers) from Jerusalem. Jesus grew up there.

Passover A week-long Jewish festival held each spring to celebrate the Jewish people's escape from slavery in Egypt.

Peacemaker A person who helps settle arguments or breaks up fights. In the Beatitudes Jesus says that people who help others not to fight are children of God.

Phylactery A small leather box worn on the forehead or arm. The box contains tiny pieces of paper with verses from the Old Testament written on them (see Deuteronomy 6:4-9). The boxes are an outward sign of the wearer's dedication to God.

Pilate The Roman ruler of Jerusalem in Jesus' time.

Place of the Skull An area outside Jerusalem where criminals were put to death. Also called Golgotha or Calvary.

Prayer Talking with, listening to God and doing things for God.

Priest A person who makes sacrificial offerings and performs other religious ceremonies.

Rabbis Teachers or leaders of the Jewish religion.

Savior A person who saves another.

Sermon A talk given to teach people how they should act.

Sin Anything you do that offends God.

Spirit of God See **Holy Spirit**.

Stable A building for animals to live in. Today most stables are made of wood, but in Jesus' time animals were often kept in caves or under the family's house.

Swaddling clothes Long, narrow bands of cloth wrapped around newborn babies to keep them snug.

Teachers Among the leaders of the Jewish religion. They are usually called *rabbis*, a word meaning teachers.

Temple A building where Jesus' people worshiped God. The Wailing Wall, what remains of the Jerusalem Temple, is still the most holy place for the Jewish people.

Tomb A cave or building for dead people.

Tongues of fire The Spirit of God looked like flames when it came down on the disciples on Pentecost.

Wedding A ceremony in which a man and a woman agree to become husband and wife and to love and take care of each other until one of them dies.

Witness A person who tells others what he or she has seen.